Manipulation
Dark Psychology

Learn the Dark Secrets of
Emotional Manipulation, Mind
Games, Undetected Mind Control,
NLP, and Psychological Warfare

By Dark Psychology Academy,
Timothy Willink

Table of Contents

Introduction

People use regularly aspects of dark psychology, especially manipulation. This is especially true of predators and the dark triad. You may find that you are manipulated in your social life, professional life, and even in your intimate relationships. But, if you have the ability to learn more about dark psychology and manipulation, then you will be able to protect yourself. Not only that, but you can learn how to avoid using manipulation tactics unknowingly, and how to use them when you intend to properly.

Within the pages of this book, you will find that you can learn everything you need about the manipulation aspects of dark psychology. This is one of the main principles of dark psychology; therefore, knowing about this aspect can greatly benefit you during your daily life. For most people, psychology is an unknown part of life. While this subject affects every moment that we live, most of us live in ignorance of how this is affecting us. Yet, if you take the opportunity to learn about dark psychology and manipulation, you can learn to benefit from it. You will gain the ability to recognize when people are attempting to manipulate you and learn how to use manipulation with little chance of failure.

Learning what you need to know, becoming more aware of dark psychology and manipulation, is as easy as reading this short book.

Thank you,

Timothy Willink

...p me, would you?" If the person says yes, then great. ...not, then respect their decision.

"It's your choice, but..."

A similar habit people may use is acting as if a choice is up to another person, even when they have already decided. They want to make it sound as if they are allowing the other person a choice, but they will be reluctant to change their mind and will try to coerce the other person into the choice they desire. This may happen when one person says the other can pick what they have for dinner, but they refuse all suggestions unless the other party chooses the only option, they are willing to eat. This type of manipulation also happens when someone says _"would you prefer we go see this movie or the other one tonight? We can see either, but I really think the first option is better."_ By saying this, they are leaving it open like a question, but still trying to get their way. Yet, it leaves the second person with little room to actually make a choice, as yours is being pushed on them. Instead, either ask the person that they would prefer with no pushing them either way or openly tell them that you would prefer and ask if that is okay with them.

"Oops, I forgot."

If you ever tell people that you "forgot" to do a task because you were tired, it was late, or you didn't feel like it then you may be manipulating those who are

Chapter 1: Are You Unknowingly Manipulating?

There are several types of manipulation, but the most commonly used purposefully, whether the person is conscious of their intent or not, is psychological manipulation. With this manipulation, emotional exploitation and mental distortion are used in order to gain privileges, benefits, control, or power all at the expense of the victim.

In a normal and healthy relationship, there is give and take, both individuals influence each other, and both help one another out. However, when one party of the relationship practices psychological manipulation, the give and take of a relationship is thrown out of balance. The victim bears an overly large burden in the relationship, all for the selfish benefit of the other person. In order to gain their desires, the manipulator will create an unhealthy balance in the relationship, all of which allows them to further manipulate their victim. This can be done in friendships, romantic relationships, parent to child, and in other types of relationships.

Few people want to consider themselves manipulative. Yet, the truth is that most of us are manipulated at various points in our life. Some people will be lucky to become manipulated rarely, and when they are, they leave with few scars. Other people are less lucky and repeatedly end up the victim of manipulative person . While we may not want to consider that we may be manipulating others ourselves, it is important to look at our behavior and ensure that we aren't, rather than hiding from an unpleasant truth. If you are manipulating people without intending to, then it is best to learn in which ways you are doing this, so that you don't unknowingly damage your relationship with those you care about.

If you ever strategically communicate subtly and in a roundabout manner to get what you want, then you may be manipulating others. This can surprise many people, as they don't realize this is what they are doing. But, if you subtly and strategically try to get your desires fulfilled, then this may be manipulation in many circumstances.

Over time, as your loved ones feel used or mistreated it can create wounds and bad blood, which is hard to overcome. You will find this is especially more difficult to overcome the longer it goes on, and if you are doing it without even realizing. The person who is manipulated repeatedly will feel hurt and resentful, and often has a difficult time forgiving the person who manipulated them.

In this chapter, we will go over some ways in which you can discover if you are unknowingly manipulating

people. Don't look away from your see the truth, or else you will be una from this. Instead, look at your action willing to truly learn if you manipulate you can then take control of your action learn the truth, you will be able to choose not you manipulate others, rather than do without knowing. This will give you healthi balanced, and stronger relationships.

"Would you like…?"

This phrase can be playful and innocent, or mor manipulative depending upon your specific relationship with a person, whether it is said joking or not, and how frequently it is used. With this example of everyday manipulation, a person will suggest that the other person may want something when they are truly the one who wants it. This may be okay if a person jokingly says *"hey, I bet you want some apple pie,"* when they are the one who wants it, but knowing that both parties fully enjoy the dessert. But it is more manipulative in other circumstances. If one person says to another *"you look like you want a drink!"* and repeatedly insisting at the other person's refusals, all the while trying to push the other person into drinking alcohol. This is obviously not respecting another person's wishes and is trying to manipulate them into something they don't want. Instead, the person should say *"I would like someone to share a drink* relying on you for these tasks. It's one thing if you live alone and you get away without doing dishes for the evening. But, if you have roommates and it is your turn to do a chore, yet you said you "forgot" because you didn't want to, then you are trying to manipulate them into letting you off the hook. This is especially problematic, as this form of manipulation often forces the burden off onto another person. Those around you are made to pick up the slack because you are dishonestly claiming to forget tasks that need to get done. Over time, people will begin to trust you less and become more easily frustrated with you, as if you are the Boy Who Cried Wolf.

"I promise!"

Promising too frequently, if you do not keep these promises, can also be manipulative. For instance, if you promise that in exchange for getting a puppy that you will handle all of its daily care but then don't live up to the promise, forcing your partner to pick up the slack. Or, someone may oversell how great an event or party is going to be because they want to go, knowing full well it isn't likely to be as wonderful as they promise. When events such as these happen, it disappoints the other person, leading them to feel angry that they were deceived. As time goes on, they are less likely to believe your promises and may begin to call you out on your habit of breaking promises.

"I'll do it myself."

Some people may push others into certain behaviors by making them feel guilty. This happens by turning themselves into a martyr and explaining phrases such as "I'll just do it myself," or "my back hurts, I'm tired and had a long day, but I guess I can make myself do the dishes." This makes the person feel guilty that you are doing the dishes and attempts to manipulate them into doing the chore for you. Instead, try to remain straightforward in what you need, and ask for help in a reasonable and fair manner without guilt trips. People will help you more willingly and happily if they aren't guilted into it.

"You're amazing!"

When you compliment people ensure that they are sincere and honest, or at the very least for the good of the other person. If you find yourself using complements to butter people up, get on their good side, and then get something for yourself, then you are manipulating their feelings for your own benefit. Some people may do this subconsciously, but it is still damaging. As time goes on, the other person is less likely to believe in any complements and will figure out that your complements aren't from a place of honestly but rather selfishness. People can begin to believe that you are insincere, contrived, and selfish.

The Silent Treatment

You can manipulate people in other ways than with your words, as well. In fact, if you tend to stop talking to people when there is conflict or if you are unhappy, then this can be manipulative. As you are giving the other person the silent treatment, they have little to no choice but to attempt to appease you. It's one thing to say "*I need a little space, can you give me time to think things over?*" but it's another to completely stop talking to someone or only give them short and tense replies to their attempts to converse.

It is okay to take time to cool off and consider the situation but ensure that you communicate that this is what you are doing. And, don't do this for an overly extended period of time or it will leave the other person at a loss. This type of manipulation may frequently come from a place of hurt, but it is important to maintain healthy communication in our relationships if we want them to last. Otherwise, we will end up losing those close to us as it will lead to resentments and more pain down the road.

Taking it Out on Others

Similar to the silent treatment, do you find yourself punishing those around you with your mood? While this is sometimes purposeful, other times, we may do it without realization. If someone tells you that you are taking out your emotions on them, then listen and take heed of their words. If we use our bad mood to guilt people or push them into behaviors that we prefer, then we are manipulating them. This will surely and slowly damage and potentially ruin relationships. Instead, if you are upset with someone to be straight forward and honest about it, willing to face your feelings, discuss the situation, overcome your emotions, and treat the other person fairly.

Chapter 2: Are You Being Manipulated?

We all have many encounters in life; some of us deal with family, friends, partners, and strangers on a daily basis. This leaves us open to being manipulated in a variety of ways and by many different people. In fact, if you have ever found yourself to be guilted, pressured, controlled, or feel that you are questioning yourself at an increased frequency, then you may be being manipulated.

It is important to know whether or not you are being manipulated and protect yourself against it, as people use manipulations to turn your own emotions and mind against you. This can become a deeply unhealthy state and can even cause people to develop a borderline personality disorder. In this chapter, we will discuss how you can recognize if you are being manipulated so that you can better protect yourself.

Whether you are being manipulated by an emotionally manipulative partner or family member or you are struggling under the pressure of an overly pushy car salesperson, you can learn how to spot various forms of manipulation. Sometimes this manipulation may appear benign, or a person can even appear friendly and kind all the while manipulating you. But this indirect and deceptive action is often abusive.

Whether someone is loudly and hostile while guilting you or flattering you while trying to deceive you and push you into actions you don't wish to take, both are manipulation. You may not realize at the moment that it is manipulation, but manipulation is most dangerous when you are unaware.

Dealing with manipulators can be especially difficult if you grew up in an abusive home with manipulative parents, siblings, or other people. People who grew up in situations such as these may become codependent, people-pleasers, or non-assertive. Due to this, they can struggle to speak up or get out of a manipulative situation, even if they feel upset and uncomfortable from the manipulation. If you think you may be one of these people, pay special attention to this chapter, as it is important for you to learn how to overcome the manipulation around you.

Tactics to Watch Out For

There are many tools and tactics that manipulators will use in daily life. While some manipulators will stick with their favorite methods, others may be a master at switching up the tactics they use to fit best and target their victim. Some of these tactics include lying, false promises, complaining, guilting, denying, blaming, fake ignorance, undermining, bribery, reversals, emotional blackmail, ultimatums, assumptions, flattery, evasiveness, sympathy, fake concern, and "forgetting."

You may find that a manipulator frequently makes assumptions about your thoughts, feelings, beliefs, and intentions. They react to these assumptions as if they were true, even if you deny their thoughts and explain your true intentions and beliefs. What you say in the conversation doesn't matter, only what the manipulator wants to believe, as they feel the need to justify their own feelings and actions. In situations such as these, the manipulator is often in denial and will refuse to see that they are, in fact, manipulating you. This circumstance happens frequently from parent to child or between partners.

As you can see, there are quite a few tactics you need to understand and watch out for, especially as these tactics can appear differently in various circumstances. Even someone well-versed in manipulation may occasionally miss signs and fall prey to a master manipulator. But, if you learn the signs and the tactics, then you can more reliably spot someone who may be manipulating you and take a step back to regain control of yourself and the situation.

Now, let's look at a few telltale signs that you may be being manipulated. Examine the interactions that leave you feeling uneasy and those you spend the most time with, to ensure that you are not missing any of these signs. It's important to remember that someone manipulators can be those closest to us, and we can be completely unaware.

You Feel Guilt, Obligation, or Fear

Oftentimes, psychological manipulation involves the components of guilt, obligation, and fear. When a person uses certain manipulation tactics, they are trying to push you into beliefs of actions that they desire, despite the fact that you most likely don't desire it. This can make you feel guilty about not following through, obligated as if you must follow their lead, or fear of the consequences if you do or don't follow through with the action.

People who use manipulation tactics that result in these feelings often act as either a bully or wear the mask of a victim. The former will make a person feel fearful as these use tools of intimidation and aggression to take a tight hold of their target. The latter portrays themselves as a victim in order to elicit guilt and a sense of obligation from their target. This individual will act hurt and can make you inner turmoil over not wanting to cause them anguish while you attempt to make your own choices. While this person may at first appear to be a victim, they are the ones using manipulation and causing harm in the relationship.

Since people are often targeted with methods, they are most likely to be trapped by, people who are targeted by the "victim" manipulators, especially struggle. These people will try to help the manipulator overcome their struggles, all while feeling responsible for helping them and spending their time and energy on the manipulator. This is just what the manipulator wants, as the victim suffers mental anguish under pressure and feels unable to make decisions that go against the desires of the manipulator.

You Question Yourself

The term *gaslighting* first originated in 1938, due to the British mystery play, titled *Gas Light*. This term refers to a type of manipulation and abuse in which a manipulator makes a person question themselves. This person may begin to question their memory, thoughts, beliefs, feelings, decisions, and even their very reality. It is a terrible form of manipulation that turns a person's mind against themselves and can affect them for years to come. A manipulator can do this by hijacking a conversation and twisting the circumstances to make you feel as though you are in the wrong until you are unable to think for yourself or remember. They often twist what you say, until you can no longer even remember what you said.

It can be difficult to spot when you are being gaslighted, as your own mind has been turned against you. But, remember that manipulators don't take responsibility. Instead they place blame on others. You may also notice that if you are being gaslighted, you feel defensive and guilty. You may believe that you have completely failed, or that you have done something wrong even if you are unsure what.

There are Always Strings Attached

If another person never does you any favors for free or out of the kindness of their heart and there are always strings attached, then they are manipulating you. These people may at first appear helpful and kind, always doing favors for people, and can, therefore, confuse those around them. Everything seems positive; you don't even realize that there is manipulation going on. But every favor or good deed that this person does is calculated, so they have expectations of what they will get in return. The manipulator will use these expectations against you, making you appear ungrateful if they don't get their "payment" for doing a good deed.

In fact, this is one of the most common types of manipulation. For instance, a person may make you feel that because they helped you when you were sick that you owe them and must, therefore, do a favor for them in turn. They may buy you a gift, only to turn around and ask you for a favor. A salesperson may do this by pushing you to buy something because you "owe" them for a deal they gave you.

While it may be normal to give and take in a relationship, each party doing favors for one another, these should be done sincerely and without strings attached.

You are Emotionally Blackmailed

Emotional blackmail isn't only manipulation; it is also a form of emotional abuse. This can include guilt, shame, intimidation, rage, and threats all so that the manipulation can reach their goal. A person may be shamed, which is meant to make them feel insecure and doubt themselves. This form can be used in many ways, such as a partner saying "you would be so beautiful if you only lost weight," or "I respect you, yet you of all people would stoop to this?" Or, they may threaten the person with warnings, accusations, and anger. This person may say something such as "If you leave me you'll never find anyone else," "you should be grateful someone would be with you when you are disabled," or "If you left me, I would kill myself." This form of manipulation doesn't only come from partners, but also friends, parents, and siblings.

Sometimes these emotional manipulators will lash out with anger, causing you to be so frightened that you are willing to sacrifice both your desires and needs. If this method fails, then they may suddenly switch to a happier and lighter mood, so that you are relieved. Once you feel safer, you are less likely to want to make them mad again, and will, therefore, agree to whatever demands the manipulator makes. If they know of anything in your past that you feel ashamed or guilty about, they may even threaten to tell other people if you don't go along with their demands.

How to Manage Manipulators

The first step to manage a manipulator is to know who you are dealing with. Remember, most manipulators will quickly learn your soft spots and triggers, so you need to learn about them in response and know their favorite tactics and go-to methods against you.

If you are in a manipulative, abusive, or dangerous relationship, then you may consider first seeking professional help. You can do this by seeing a therapist who can personally help you or contacting the National Domestic Violence Hotline (1-800-799-7233). At the very least, try to find a group of supportive people. This can either be an official support group or simply a friend or two who you can vent to and get perspective and advice from. Remember, if you are in a toxic and abusive relationship, you have been conditioned to believe that your interactions are normal and just the way things are. But this is not true. You need to learn to break away from the idea that abuse is just something to live with and get through.

Try to create boundaries with those who are manipulating you, to help keep their manipulation at a distance and lower its effects. Often, people who use manipulation attempt to break down boundaries, but you need to fight to keep these in place. It is important for every relationship and every person to have boundaries, and you are not in the wrong for keeping these. You can make your own decisions, have your own feelings, and think your own thoughts without your manipulator taking them under their control.

If you are directly manipulated at the moment, keep in mind that you can delay and hold off on any response. For instance, if the manipulator wants you to make a quick decision you don't have to, instead, you can insist that you have the time to sleep on it. Don't sign any legal contracts without the time to go over them with a lawyer and fully read them, either. Whatever the case, it is vital that you aren't pushed into making an irreversible decision too quickly. Take the time you need to think and do what you truly feel you want and need.

Lastly, if you have been manipulated for a long time or grew up in a home full of manipulation, you will most likely have a more difficult time breaking free of these approaches. In order to do this, you must spend your time learning to increase your self-esteem, self-respect, boundaries, assertiveness, and tools for defense. You can do this by yourself and with the help of certain self-help books but having a therapist who can personalize your approach is incredibly helpful and a wise option to take.

Chapter 3: Ways in Which People Are Manipulated

There are many ways in which people are manipulated. In fact, there are so many methods of manipulation; it is hard to keep track of them. Therefore, we will spend this chapter looking at some of the most common ways people use manipulation.

1. They Act as Though They Are Above You

There are those who are arrogant, egotistical, and narcissistic. This is especially true of the dark triad within dark psychology, in which narcissists are known to commonly believe and act as though they are above and better than everyone else.

When this type of manipulation occurs, the person may treat you as if you are a child or incapable of thinking or acting for yourself. This is combined with condescending comments and body language to send the message that you are inferior to them.

This may include phrases such as "you're ridiculous," "don't be stupid," or "it's not a big deal; you need to calm down."

2. Jokes at Your Expense

Often, this type of manipulation is a form of emotional abuse that is carried out in front of an audience. This is because while it may be somewhat effective when said solely to you, these jokes are especially harmful when they are said in front of an audience. This can include making fun of you in any way in order to humiliate you, either in-person or online.

A person, especially an abusive partner, may say something such as *"I thought I was marrying someone hot, but then I married her and she took the makeup off,"* all while laughing. Some people may even wear a shirt saying "I'm with fatty" when going out with their spouse. These may seem drastic, as they are abusive, but sadly they are all too common. If the person on the receiving end of this gets visibly upset, they are chastised and told that they *"can't take a joke."*

3. Staring Daggers

There is much subtle body language that can only be deciphered by an expert. But people will often use obvious body language with the intent purpose of sending a message to their target. This body language is often meant to make the target feel uncomfortable, guilty, or fearful. This may include body language such as eye rolling, staring daggers, extended eye contact that doesn't include words or blinking, condescending head tilts, raising one eyebrow, angry expression, condescendingly looking over the glasses, shaking the head, judgmental expressions, looks of disgust, smug smirking or grinning.

This type of manipulation is never used alone, as it is always a single aspect of a larger plan. Alone, this body language could simply be a miscommunication. Therefore, this is often paired with words that match the body language and other manipulative actions.

4. Bullying Behavior

Someone who bullies uses a combination of various manipulation techniques. This often involves acting in a threatening, aggressive, and hostile manner. When you are affected by bullying, you feel scared and attempt to walk on eggshells in order to avoid the person's explosive anger. These bullies can use tones of voice, abusive phrases, body language, the threat of social consequences, and even threat of physical violence in order to get their way. When people encounter this bullying behavior, they either tend to avoid the bully as much as possible or suck up to them to get on their good side.

5. Physical Intimidation

If someone is bigger than you, they may try to use their size to physically intimidate you. Even if they never directly say or act like they are going to hit you, they may come to stand right up next to you and literally look down on you so that you feel them towering over you. This is especially common for men to do to women, as they are on average taller. People may also use this method against kids frequently, as they are also short in height.

6. Yelling

Yelling may be used in order to not only manipulate but also intimidate others. While the volume of a person's voice may not improve their argument, it does scare a person and dominate the conversation so that the other person cannot get a word in.

In response, the person who is being yelled at will naturally raise their voice to defend themselves and feel as if they are on even footing. But the manipulator will then use this as another excuse to get mad at their target.

7. Guilt Tripping

Manipulators love using guilt trips, especially against people who are more sensitive and kind-hearted, as they have a tough time fighting back against this manipulation. Even if these people put up a fight, they often leave the conversation feeling extreme guilt and may later cave into the manipulator's desires. This can include a manipulator using phrases such as *"I thought we were friends," "I can't believe you," "I thought I could count on you, but I guess I was wrong,"* or *"I've done so much for you and you won't even help me?"* Not only do partners, friends, and family use guilt-tripping, but it is a favorite method used by charities trying to raise money. Think about all those sad animal shelter commercials with the emotional music playing in the background; they are trying to guilt trip you into donating.

8. Playing with Your Emotions

Emotional manipulation tells a person exactly what they do or don't want to hear in order to elicit the desired response. A manipulator may tell their target that they love them or that they hate them. They may act in a way to make their target fall into despair or become full of jealousy. Whatever the manipulator wants, they know how to draw out these emotions in those around them.

A person may yell at their partner and tell them that they hate them, in hopes of gaining the submission of the other person and their desired action, whether they want the other to agree to go along with something or to give them a gift.

9. Passive Aggressive

When someone acts passive aggressive, they are manipulating you in ways that may be less obvious to some, but it is often strongly felt by the person it is directed toward. A person can act passive aggressive in many ways, especially when they are trying to pretend to the world that they are in the right. Some of the methods that may be used include the silent treatment, agreeing to do something and then purposefully doing a bad job, purposefully making things difficult, "forgetting" to do tasks, disguised insults, playing dumb, sarcasm, negative body language, and more.

10. Withholding Validation, Approval, Love, or Sex

A typical favorite tool of the manipulator is only to conditionally accept a person. A parent, child, friend, or partner may withhold validation, approval, love, or sex unless you act in a specific way or go along with strict requests. Any approval these people give you has strings attached, and they will take it away if you don't act under their control.

That habit works well on people who have a habit of seeking approval, and therefore it is most successful on people who are young, those who have been deprived of love, who are in a state of emotional weakness, or those who were abused in the past.

11. Faux Time Constraints

In order to put people under pressure and restrict them from time to make a wise decision people will sometimes use false time constraints. For instance, a boss may tell their employees that there is a tight deadline with a customer or a specific project, only for it to later be discovered that they had lied and there was no time constraint. However, while business frequently uses this tactic, this does not only happen in professional settings.

12. Harming Someone's Image

If a person is unable to control you, then they may try to harm your public image. They can do this by telling lies to those who have yet to meet you or even your friends who they suspect are disloyal. They may do this by calling you a liar, telling people you are selfish or weaving elaborate storylines of things you never did. These people can be caught though when they mix up their lies and begin to forget what they originally said. This type of manipulation frequently happens in abusive relationships, but also in politics. You will see some politicians calling each other names, which is only meant to taint the view of the public despite having little to no substance behind them.

13. Peer Pressure

Some people will know you don't want to do something and will therefore try to force you into it with peer pressure. For instance, they will try to make you drink and encourage everyone else to push you into drinking as well. They may propose marriage to you in a large crowd so that everyone is looking on waiting for the answer to be "yes."

Or, they may also do it by holding your opinions against that of others. Saying stuff such as *"are you the one that is right while everyone else is wrong?"* or *"you are the only person who thinks like this!"* This method is frequently used by abusive partners and friends.

There are many types of manipulation; it can come in many shapes and sizes. Just because you are familiar with one or two types of manipulation doesn't mean that there could be many more affecting you in your daily life. Consider this list and how it may apply to different situations and people in your life to get a full picture.

Chapter 4: Protect Yourself from Manipulation

We have discussed many ways in which people manipulate. As there are so many different ways to manipulate there are many different ways in which to protect yourself. Depending upon the type of manipulation you are being affected by you may need to switch up your approach to counter the manipulation. In this chapter, we will go over many ways you can protect yourself, whether the manipulation is being brought about by a family member, partner, friend, coworker, or anyone else.

Firstly, ensure that you are careful not to fall into the trap that manipulators lay in your wait. They will enjoy toying with your mind and emotions. They will interrogate and blame you, send you into a state of confusion and fear, and more. If you find yourself frequently dealing with these people, especially if it is the same person time and again, be careful not to allow them to take you by surprise. Whether it is your partner or coworker, don't allow them to anger you or guilt you, instead either ignore them or act as if nothing has happened. Remember, it is the manipulator's intent to throw you off balance, so don't allow them to succeed. Over time, as they continue to fail to get a rise out of you, they may give up. Although, they also may move onto new tactics, so stay on your feet to ensure that they do not win the battle. But, even if they do win the battle, you can try again and win the war.

If you have an especially tricky situation, such as with a manipulative and abusive partner or parent, you may consider writing down important conversations in a notebook or on your phone. If possible, you may even record them on your phone. This may seem extreme, but it can literally save you in abusive situations. This helps as if the person is gaslighting you and trying to change your perception of yourself and reality it will allow you to stay anchored to reality. Write down both your true thoughts and the manipulations said, as this will allow you to remember the truth and the abuse the other person is causing. If a situation is especially abusive, you can use audio recordings of conversations later on, if you decide to seek help, as people are more likely to believe you if you provide them with proof.

Whenever possible, try to completely avoid people who are manipulating you. This can sometimes be difficult, as not all manipulators reveal themselves from the beginning. But, if you keep the tactics mentioned in this book in mind, then you can watch out for them in your personal life. If you have a bad feeling about someone, don't hesitate to keep your distance until you decide whether or not you can trust them. If you live or work with a manipulator, you may be unable to avoid them completely, but try to limit your interactions as you are able. You will find that the more you are able to limit these interactions, the better you will feel both mentally and spiritually, giving you more energy for the important aspects of your life.

If you are constantly dealing with a person's manipulation, then you may need to confront them. Some people are able to manipulate those around them so well that they are never called out on it, and therefore think they can get away with it. If someone is repeatedly making you uncomfortable, try to stand up for yourself. This isn't always possible to do, especially if someone shows indications of possibly getting physical, so be sure that you do it in a safe location and with a person who you don't believe will physically harm you. At the very least, you can try to call them out when there is another person present. By doing this, even if they don't stop the behavior completely, you can be proud of yourself for standing up for yourself, someone else, or the truth. It may not change things immediately, but if you and other people begin to call someone out on their behavior, they may slowly change as they see more people aren't willing to put up with them anymore.

If you are entering a new relationship, keep an eye out for abusive or manipulative behaviors. If these people refuse to take responsibility, begin to steamroll your opinions, take their anger out on you, withhold affection when angry, or any other manipulative behaviors, then allow yourself to take a step back. You don't want to continue deepening a relationship with a potentially harmful person. Try to keep the relationship in a neutral position until you can determine if the person simply made a mistake on a bad day, or if it is a habit that they are unlikely to break. There is nothing wrong with taking a step back from a relationship, especially as manipulators are prevalent and always on the lookout for their next target.

Manipulators are also master liars, so don't feel that if you have someone you full well know is attempting to manipulate you that you are required to have to accept their apology. If these people manipulated you and treated you poorly and are now apologizing in a way that seems fake, you don't have to accept it. If you want, you can tell them that you forgive them, but that doesn't mean that you have to allow them back into your life or give them the same level of trust they previously held. If them, or anyone else, is upset at your refusal to allow them back into your good graces you can simply remind them that trust has to be earned and they haven't earned it back yet.

Manipulators always like to have the spotlight on themselves. If you are struggling to walk with a sprained ankle, they will complain about the time they had a headache. If you are struggling to breathe through an asthma attack, they will tell you the time they had a cancer scare. Their stories may be true, or they may not, but it doesn't matter as they are only using them as a way to invalidate your struggles and pain. Don't let these taunts get into your head, remember: all pain and suffering are valid; life isn't a competition of "who has it worse." If at all possible, try to shut down the other person's taunts and walk away, or at the very least ignore them.

Try to strengthen your resolve and mentality. It can be easy to let a master manipulator into your head, after all, they have had much practice. But, if you let their outbursts, insults, guilt trips, and other tactics get into your head, then you will begin to fall under their spell. Instead, try to entertain their tirades without internalizing what they are saying. You can later laugh it off or vent your frustration to a friend. Remind yourself of who you are, that you are strong, you have self-worth, there is no need for you to rely on a person who is trying to manipulate you. This is most easily done if you give yourself frequent positive talks. When you find yourself down try to restore your image of yourself by using positive self-affirmations and reminding yourself of the truth that the manipulator is lying about. This will help you overcome their lies and manipulations while maintaining a strong mind.

Lastly, remember that manipulators do not want to be held accountable. You may feel like you want to talk through an argument and come to a resolution, but it is unlikely to be successful. The manipulator is only likely to use this as an opportunity to find a way in which they can better manipulate you, your perception of them, or the perception of others. You can confront a manipulator, but don't feel that it is your job to make them see how they have hurt you and hold their hand while they change their ways.

Chapter 5: How to Use Dark Psychology Manipulation

While predators and those in the dark triad certainly use manipulation tactics quite frequently, you don't have to be a predator or toxic person in order to learn some techniques. Some forms of manipulation are more damaging while others are simple forms of persuasion that are safer to use. These can be especially helpful to use when there is a predator interfering with your daily life. Using these techniques, you can pacify the predator, or at the very least get them to back off and leave you or a person you are protecting alone. For instance, if you see a teenager being bullied by some people older than them, then you can stand up for them by using a few manipulation techniques on the bullies.

These techniques can even help you in some jobs, such as sales jobs, advertising, police work, and working as an agent at a government agency. With using a few techniques, you can help protect yourself, defend the weak, and excel in your career. But remember, these techniques only work if the person doesn't know you are manipulating them, so you have to be careful in the way you go about it.

It is natural and a good sign of a healthy conscience if you feel guilty when using these techniques on others.

Yet, it can be important sometimes when you or someone else is getting walked all over, manipulated, or bullied. You don't have to use these techniques every day or carelessly, but they are helpful to know if you ever need to protect yourself or others.

Be sure that you use manipulation techniques wisely, as well. If you begin to use them in your healthy relationships with others, you will soon find your relationship degrading. They will lose their trust in you and have increasing anxiety whenever they are near you.

Learn Body Language

Learning how to manipulate people (and know when you are being manipulated) requires knowing a certain amount of body language. You need to be able to not only read the body language of another person but also portray specific body language yourself. This is a normal part of communication that has been passed down from generation to generation in ever animal species, including humans. This non-verbal communication can clue you in when a person is lying when they are hiding something or allow you to decipher anything else they may be feeling.

Our natural communication with body language is nearly uncontrollable. Even people who are well-versed in body language will find themselves accidentally communicating things they intended to keep hidden if they lose their focus. This is because it is a natural way in which the brain both communicates and reads the communication of others. It can tell us much about those around us without words. Have you ever had a bad gut feeling about someone, but were unsure why? This is likely due to their body language. Your brain is picking up on their body language and knows it is off, but as this is subconscious you are unable to place what it is that discomforts you. With body language you can learn to understand things about a person without the use of words. In the same way, you can communicate without words, or use body language in addition to words to get your message across.

Some people say the phrase "ninety percent of communication is non-verbal." This may sound like an exaggeration, but the opposite is true. In fact, a shocking ninety-three percent of communication is non-verbal! This means that everyday communication of yours can be thrown off if you aren't communicating what you want with your body language. For instance, you may feel uncomfortable in a job interviewer, but you would never tell the interviewer that! Yet, your body language may be conveying this very thought if you have your arms crossed or keep looking down. Instead, you want to portray body language that is confident but not cocky.

If you hope to convey body language well, you also need to know how to read the body language of other people. This subject could cover a whole book, so I suggest you read one on the matter, but there are basics you can learn in the meantime. This is important, as you may think a person's words are kind, but then if you learn their body language, you can find that they are actually portraying feelings of dismissal and may be hiding something. As you are not an expert in the field, you are unable to take these signs as fact, but it can be a helpful insight.

You will find that the more you practice reading the body language of other people, the better you are at showing the body language you intend.

A few body languages tips you should remember include:

Mimic the positive emotions of other people in order to create more positive feelings and agreement. For instance, if the other person is nodding their head then you nod your head, as well. If the other person is sitting in a relaxed position, you mirror what they are doing. But, keep this centered on only positive body language, as if you mimic negative body language is a situation such as a job interview then you will create the opposite effect of what you want.

People naturally hide their hands when they have something to hide. Therefore, if you want to feel trusted talk with your palms open as if you are bearing all for people to see. You will often see people using upward-facing gestures with their palms when they are telling a story or giving a speech; this is because they are trying to convey knowledge, they know to be true. Try to mimic this behavior.

- If a group of people is laughing, then the people who first lock eye contact during the laugh most likely trust each other the most. If you are trying to build a stronger relationship with someone, then when you are sharing a laugh with them, and others are sure to look them in the eye. But, do this naturally, don't just stare them in the eyes while you laugh. People often close their eyes or look upward when they laugh before looking at the person they are laughing with.

- When people shake hands, the hands are rarely perfectly parallel. Instead, one hand is slightly on top with the other on the bottom. This may seem insignificant, but the hand on the top and facing downward is asserting dominance, whereas the hand on the bottom and facing upwards is showing submission.

Change Perspectives

One of the most important aspects of manipulation is having a plan. You want to think ahead about what you do and don't want to communicate with the person. One aspect of this is learning what perspective you want to share with a person and ensuring that you plan out how to best communicate this perspective with tact and important phrases.

For instance, if you watch popular cooking shows you will see that chefs tell the story of their food and create the perspective that people hold about it. A chef wants a person salivating over the food, rushing to either taste it or make the dish themselves. In order to do this, they use language that induces hunger and allows a person to imagine the flavors, all while highlighting the best possible aspects of a dish. You will never catch a professional chef that is good at talking to the camera say something such as *"my dish has lemon to accent the shrimp, although I may have added too much spice. I hope you enjoy spicy foods"* while nervously chuckling. This is only something an amateur to communicating to a camera would ever do. Instead, the professional would spin everything in a positive light. They would discuss the zesty lemon, the succulent shrimp, the fresh herbs, the luscious butter, and the spicy pepper. All the while, they wouldn't discuss the spice as if it were a bad thing. Instead, they would comment on how anyone who loves a burst of flavor or traditional Caribbean food would fall in love at first bite.

In the same way, you would never hear a car salesperson discuss the bad aspects of a car in a negative light. Even if you ask them about something and it isn't the best aspect of a vehicle, they will turn it into something positive before redirecting you to a stronger sales point.

When doing this, it is important that you don't lie, rather that you look at the glass as half full and reveal the hidden potential of whatever perspective you are communicating. This way, the other person can see that you are telling the truth and believe in your word, allowing them to see the same perspective as you hope to communicate.

Focus not only on words you are using, but the phrases, tone of voice, context, emotion, and body language. Think through these aspects, considering how you need to structure your conversation to give the best delivery. In order to communicate a given subject to a specific person, do you need to appeal to their sense of emotion or logic? Are the words convincing you, or do they sound fake? Do you know what you are talking about, or are you making it up as you go along? Are you thinking outside of the box or using common clichés?

Leverage Your Knowledge

In order to manipulate people, you need to understand them. This involves both general human needs and what individuals need. For instance, humans in general desire connection. But, some individuals, in particular, may desire this connection more than others, depending on their background and personality. Other people may desire affection, conformity, the ability to stand out from the crowd, a listening ear, acceptance, and more. While all humans have basic needs we need to understand, it is also important to know what each individual need.

You can use this knowledge to convince a person or press their buttons. For instance, if you see a person bullying another, you may be able to goad them into taking a bet with you if you can tell that they are a risk taker. This way, if you win the bet, you can get them to leave the other person alone.

By knowing a person's individual weaknesses, you can use your strengths to control a situation and conversation. Even the strongest of people have their weaknesses. It may take time to see what an individual's weaknesses are, but if you take the time to study people in your daily life, then you will find that it gets easier to quickly spot these weaknesses. The more you learn about their weaknesses, the more you will understand them as an individual, their thought processes, their body language tendencies, their characteristics, and more.

The biggest key to success in manipulation is having knowledge. This includes knowledge of people, individuals, and communication. Not only should you gain this knowledge of others, but also of yourself. Understand your own weaknesses, body language tendencies, and more. This will allow you to better communicate and prevent yourself from falling into manipulation.

When trying to change a person's perspective, know that no matter how much they rationalize their thought process it is their emotions that cause them to desperately cling to it. Therefore, if you want them to get closer to your perspective, you need to understand what is emotionally driving them. Then, after you know them you can learn how to communicate your position in a way that touches on the emotions that are important to them for the most success.

Chapter 6: Tips and Tricks

You have learned a lot about the dark psychology of manipulation. But, no matter how much you learn, there is always more you can learn about this subject. This is because everyone is different, and therefore every person can be manipulated in a different way or will choose to manipulate others in a new way. But the more time you spend analyzing the pages of this book as well as the people around you the better you will come to understand how to avoid being manipulated and how to manipulate better. Take these tips and tricks to heart in order to improve upon your technique.

1. Work with a Person's Emotions

You can best manipulate a person if you are working with their emotions, not against them. You see this all the time on TV and in advertisements. Imagine, an advertising agency doesn't sell a product by going against what their audience believes. A submarine sandwich shop isn't going to sell their product by trying to convince people that they hate pizza. Instead, they are going to highly the best parts about their product that people will like, that will play into their emotions.

2. Own Your Emotions

You are unable to manipulate others or overcome manipulation if you don't have a handle on your own emotions. If you are easy to read and let all of your emotions be freely communicated, either by words or body language, then you are making yourself a target.

Consider, if you are pranking someone in order to scare them and trick them into thinking that there is a scary apparition behind them, you don't laugh while telling them. If you are laughing, then they will know that what you are saying and the way you are acting aren't matching up. Instead, you yourself should act scared, as if you are worried you are about to get your life taken away. They will buy into the fear you are portraying and then become scared themselves. The same is true of when you are manipulating someone. Own your emotions and then take control over them so that you can portray the emotions you need to in order to succeed.

3. Create Trust

It is difficult to trust people, especially for those who have been abused or manipulated in the past. In this case, you need to create trust between you and another person. There are different ways in which you can do this, such as with body language. But, one really successful way is to open up and talk about something personal. For instance, you could talk about a painful story from your past. This will help the other person to better connect with you and create a deeper sense of trust more quickly.

4. Be Likable

People aren't likely going to be manipulated by you if they don't like you. Think about it; you likely aren't manipulated by politicians of a party you hate. Just as liberals are rarely manipulated by Republican tactics, Republicans are rarely manipulated by liberal tactics. Instead, politicians don't try to manipulate people outside their party, but their very own party. They know they can't win with the opposition, but they can with people who share similarities with them and are more likely to buy into their portrayal. Therefore, make yourself likable. This can mean a different approach depending on who you are trying to manipulate. But, in general, you want to smile and show positive and open body language. Be kind, share a kind word, open up to them, and they will soon find themselves liking you.

5. Act the Role of the Victim

This manipulation tactic can be tricky, as it is easily spotted if it is overused, and some people spot it more quickly than others. In fact, people hate it when they realize someone is playing the victim so it can backfire. But, if you do it successfully, it can really work. Just be careful when you try this method and don't use it around the same people frequently. This method is often most successful when the other person feels guilty.

6. Try Bribery

When manipulating you don't bribe with money, but rather with material goods, mental rewards, or emotional rewards. This changes widely from person to person but find whatever will best reward and persuade a person in order to reward them. For instance, a person may be bribed with attention, acceptance, or help around the house with chores. Whatever it is, find it.

7. Don't be Afraid to Flirt

Women know that this trick works all too well, simply play up your charms and flirt. Of course, you don't want to use this against everyone, but if you know which people to flirt with and which to charm instead, then you can find a good balance when manipulating. This approach is especially helpful for people who lack self-esteem or are lonely. Women often use this method in order to protect themselves. If they are around a man who they are scared of, they may act charming until he lets his guard down and they can get to safety.

8. Don't Act Manipulative

This may sound contradictory, but many beginners make the mistake of continuing to attempt to manipulate a person after they have been caught. You don't want to do this. Instead, back off, act calm, and allow the other individual to regain control of the situation. This will make them doubt themselves.

Conclusion

Manipulation has many purposes. While you can certainly use it for darker purposes, you can also use it in order to be a better salesperson, excelling in police work, read people better, excel in your social life, and much more. But whether you choose to use manipulation for charitable deeds or for more nefarious means, you have learned the tools you need in this book to help you succeed.

Take it slowly and don't be discouraged if it takes time. There are many tools for manipulation, and none of them can be mastered overnight. Just as Rome wasn't built in a day, you can't master reading body language, communicating through body language, controlling your tone of voice, reading peoples' weaknesses, hiding your emotions, and the many different manipulation tactics all in one day. Give yourself time, and as you steadily put in the effort to learn, you will find yourself climbing to new heights.

FREE BONUS

P.S. Is it okay if we overdeliver?

I believe in overdelivering way beyond our reader's expectations. Is it okay if I overdeliver?

Here's the deal, I am going to give you an extremely valuable cheatsheet of "Accelerated Learning"...

What's the catch? I need to trust you... You see, my team and I wants to overdeliver and in order for us to do that, we've to trust our reader to keep this bonus a secret to themselves. Why? Because we don't want people to be getting our ultimate accelerated learning cheatsheet without even buying our books itself. Unethical, right?

Ok. Are you ready?

Simply Visit this link:
http://bit.ly/acceleratedcheatsheet

Everything else will be self explanatory after you've visited: http://bit.ly/acceleratedcheatsheet

We hope you'll enjoy our free bonuses as much as we've enjoyed preparing it for you!

Free Preview of "Time Management" by Timothy Willink

How to Get the Most Out of this Book

Time management is something that all of us can benefit from. It helps us to get things done more efficiently and without feeling so stressed out from falling behind. When you utilize the right time management techniques, you are going to be able to get a ton of things done, and still, have time to spend with friends and family.

This guidebook is going to take some time to talk about the different things that you need to know to get started with your own time management journey. The best way that you can get the most out of this book includes

1. Figure out the root causes of why you are struggling with managing your time well.
2. Decide which method of time management you would like to use to see better results.
3. Try each method that you want to work with one at a time. See how it improves your time management skills, and work from there.

Chapter 1: What Does Time Management Mean?

Time management is going to refer to the development of tools and processes that help you to increase the amount of productivity and efficiency that you want to have. This can be a desirable thing in business, as well as in your personal life.

It helps you to get more done throughout the day, reducing the amount of time that it takes to get your work done. This makes you more productive and helps you to leave your work back at the office while you enjoy more of what you enjoy in your personal life.

Today, the idea of time management has really broadened out to help cover your personal life as well as your working lives. And if you can use time management in the proper manner, you will be able to improve your work-life balance, and your happiness in the process.

The theory, though, is not something that is universally accepted. For example, they may think that there really isn't a thing like a work-life balance because there is work, there is life, and there isn't a way to balance them.

But no matter what you are doing, time management is able to help you to get things done, without messing around and procrastinating all the time.

How many times have you wasted time at work and then at the end of the day, you feel like you have to rush through all of your work at the end of the day, or even take it home and miss out on free time or time with your family?

When you allow this to happen on a regular basis, you are going to feel miserable. Your stress levels are going to go through the roof. Even though you technically have a lot of time to get the work done, you will save it to the end, and feel strained and stressed the whole time.

Time management can help you avoid this issue. You will be able to get your work done on time, with even free time left over at the end of the day to help you relax and feel better when your day is over.

A History of Time Management

The roots of all time management were in business. During the 19th century, the industrial revolution started, and factories needed to be able to fabricate a brand-new relationship with time.

Factory work, unlike the agrarian labor from before, demanded punctuality. People had to learn how to live by a clock and the time on it, rather than by the sun.

Schooling became as much, or more, about preparing students so that they could do well in a factory and have the right habits along the way. And the overall goal that comes with this is being punctual and productivity.

When it came to a factory, working and fitting as much as possible into the workday was so important. Remember that when it came to business, time is money. If workers could be on time and get more done during the day, they were more valuable to the business.

Personal Time Management

Although the original ideas of time management were brought about to help in factories and to make good workers, it is possible to use time management on your own.

You can use it to ensure that you get as much done during the day as possible. Or you can use it in a way to ensure that you can actually get the work that you need to be done during the day, both at home and at work.

Today, when we start to think about time management and what it is all about, most of us are going to think about it in more of a personal manner.

Personal time management is defined as a way to manage your time so that you waste less of it doing the things that you have to get done. This allows you to have more time to do some of the things that you would enjoy doing.

Time management is going to be presented to us as a set of skills. The idea here is that once you can master these skills, you are going to be more efficient, organized, and overall happier.

Whether you believe that this is able to help you or not, a working person definitely benefits from honing even a few of these time management skills so that they can get more work done during the day, and have more free time in the end.

There are quite a few different personal management skills that you can concentrate on. Some of the different personal time management skills that you should know include

1. Scheduling
2. Delegating
3. Decision making
4. Prioritizing
5. Planning
6. Goal setting

Many people find that work with these kinds of skills, as well as some of the tool for time management like phone apps and PIM software, can ensure that they can manage your time in a more effective manner.

For example, you may choose to work with a calendar app. This kind of app will help you to schedule out things and keep track of different events and appointments.

Whether you use technological time management tools, or you prefer to stick with pen and paper, the first step when you are working with time management is to analyze how you currently spend your time. Then, decide what needs to change for your success.

All of us want to be able to get all our work done. We are tired of feeling stressed out at work, and like we are not able to get things done on time. And we dream about a time when were able to go home and hang out with our spouse and our kids, or even with some friends, and enjoy them, without having to get work done on top of it all.

This is exactly what time management is able to do for us. It helps us to learn the best way to manage our time, so we get the most things done, especially the things that are the most important.

Time management is going to work for everyone. Whether you want to get work done at home, you need to finish a big project, or some other aspect of your life, time management is the tool that you need to finally get it done!

Chapter 2: Setting Your Goals

In your life, you will find that setting goals and practicing time management techniques are two necessary elements. These can help you reach success. Many people feel like they are adrift in the world. They work hard, but they don't seem to get anywhere that is worthwhile, no matter how hard they try.

A key reason that they feel this way is that they haven't spent enough time thinking about what they want out of life and haven't set themselves form goals. After all, it doesn't make sense for you to set out on a new journey without a good idea of where you are going.

Setting goals is an important thing that you can do when it is time to work on your time management skills. It is hard to manage your time. There are always a lot of distractions, and you don't want to miss out on things. Plus, a lot of times the work is boring, and we want to figure out how to avoid it

When you learn how to utilize the time management techniques that are available to you, it is a lot easier to get all of that work done, and you can enjoy more of your free time.

So, with this in mind, it is time to take a look at the steps that you need to take to help set goals. First, you need to consider what you would like to achieve, and then commit yourself to it.

The best kinds of goals are SMART goals. Specific, measurable, attainable, relevant, and time-bound (SMART). These kinds of goals are going to motivate you, and you can write them down in order to make them more tangible.

From there, you can plan the steps that you must take to realize your goal and cross off each one as you start to work through them all.

You will find that goal setting can be a really powerful process when it is time to think about your ideal future. And you can use these goal setting to help motivate yourself to turn your vision of this future into reality.

From here, we want to learn how to set the goals that we want. The process of setting goals is going to help you better choose where you want to go in your life. When you know the precise thing that you want to achieve, you know where you should concentrate your efforts. It also helps you to find when the distractions are going to come up, so you can avoid them and stay on track.

Why should I set goals?
It is so important in many aspects of your life, to set certain goals to help you get where you want.

Everyone who is successful, from business owners, athletes and other top achieves in their fields will all set goals, and you should do it as well.

Setting goals will help you to get the motivation that you need over the short term and provides you with long-term vision. It is going to focus your acquisition of knowledge and makes it easier for you to organize your time and resources so that you stop wasting both and can get the most out of your life.

When you learn how to set clearly defined and sharp goals, it is easier to measure out your progress, and take some pride in your achievement of these goals. In addition, you will see the progress you make, even when it all seems pointless. Setting goals is going to raise your self-confidence, as you start to recognize your own ability and competence to achieve the goals that you have set.

How to set your personal goals

You can set your own goals based on a few different levels including:

1. First, you need to go through and set your own big picture, the idea of what you would like to do with your life over the next ten years or more, and then you will be able to identify the large-scale goals that you would like to achieve.
2. From here, you can break these down into some smaller targets, the things that you want to meet in order to reach your own goals.

3. You will now have a plan, and you will be able to work in order to achieve these goals.

This is why we want to start out this whole process by setting goals by looking at your lifetime goals. Then, when you start to work on this and get to the things that you can do in shorter amounts of time, such as a week, a month, and a year, you can start to make progress towards your goals.

So, our first step with this one is to figure out what we want to do. Since we are working with time management, you want to take this goal to help you to get through your procrastination and do better with your time management.

That is the overreaching goal, the thing that you want to use to help you actually get the work done without feeling so stressed out or having to worry about bringing the work home with you. Maybe that is your overall goal to work with over the next year.

But that brings up the question of how you will be able to make this happen. It is great to have a goal of working on time management and getting more done through the day. From here, you need to be able to figure out the steps that you can take actually to make that happen.

Once you have come up with your big goal, you need to set up a bunch of smaller goals that you can do to help you reach this. This is going to be different based on what techniques work for you, and how bad your time management skills are.

Maybe over the next six months, you want to implement one technique into your schedule each month and see how it does. But at the end of the six months, you may be utilizing six different techniques to help you get your work done faster than before so you can reduce some of the stress that you have.

For example, maybe during the first month, you are going to concentrating on doing some scheduling and prioritizing what items need to be done first during the day. In the second month, you will learn how to reduce some of the distractions that make getting work done difficult. And the third month you work with the timer model to see how much you can do in that time frame.

And then you just keep going from there. you can even create a to-do list to help you remember what parts of the process you want to reach by different times.

In the beginning, you may notice that these smaller steps may seem small and silly, but they are going to help you to reach your overall goal of being better at time management.

Before you implement this whole plan, take a look over the big goal, and all the little steps. Are the steps manageable and are you really able to keep up with the schedule that you set? You want to make the goals attainable, but not so easy that you will be done in a few days and get bored.

Once the plan is ready, it is time to move forward. Start with each part and see what you need to do to make it work for your needs.

The way that you set the goals in your life is going to depend on where you started, and how far you would like to go. Some people can jump right on this and see some great results with their time management, and they will see results in just a few weeks with some of the techniques in this guidebook.

Others may run into some struggles and find that it takes a bit longer. You will find that even implementing one or two of these different techniques will improve your time management skills and will ensure that you can get more done during the day.

Staying on the Course

Once you have decided what your goal should be and what you would like to have as your first set of goals. You will then need to make sure that you stay on the course, and don't give up the goals that you had set.

Keep the process going by reviewing and updating your goals and making the changes that you need on a daily basis. You can also take a look over the longer term plans and make modifications as needed to ensure that any of the experiences or priorities that you have are reflected in this as much as possible.

A good way to help you review your longer-term plan and to make sure that it always matches up with your views includes scheduling regular and repeating reviews using a computer-based diary. Set up an appointment with yourself and stick with it.

SMART Goals

Before we move on to some of the techniques that you can do with setting goals, we first need to take a closer look at the idea of making SMART goals. This will ensure that you are setting goals that work for you, and goals that you can actually achieve, even if it takes some hard work.

SMART is going to be a mnemonic device that helps us know more about how we can set our goals. SMART is going to stand for

1. Specific: You need to make sure that your goals are specific.
2. Measurable: Your goals need to be ones that you can measure.
3. Attainable: You want to have a bit of a challenge with the goals that you reach for, but they still need to be ones that you can reach.
4. Relevant: This one is sometimes known as rewarding. It is meant to help to pick out the

goals that mean the most to you and will provide you with the biggest reward when you are done with them.

5. Time-bound: You can't just set goals and hope it all works out for the best. You have to add a timestamp to your goals to help you actually achieve them.

Let's look at an example of how you can make this work. You may have a goal of sailing around the world. This is a good goal, but it becomes more powerful when you turn it into a SMART goal. You may say something like, "I want to complete my trip around the world by November 22, 2030."

Some other tips that you can follow to help you set your goals and actually reach them include:

1. State them in a positive manner. You want to make sure that your goals are expressed in a positive manner.

2. Be precise: Your goals need to be precise. If you can add amounts, times, and dates, this makes them easier to measure. It helps you to know exactly when you have achieved the goal or not.

3. Set your priorities. When you are going with a few goals, it is best to give each one a priority. This can help you to avoid feeling overwhelmed with too many goals and will help you to focus on the ones that are the most important.

4. Write them down. Nothing is more effective in goal setting than writing things down.

5. Keep the goals small: You can have one big goal but split it up into smaller parts so that you can measure the progress you are making.

6. Set goals that are realistic: These need to be realistic to you. You do not have the same talents, resources, and time as others. Set your goals so that they will push you forward a bit and won't be too easy, but you don't want to make them impossible either.

Setting goals is going to be one of the most important things that you can do in your life. It will help you to get things to work out the way that you want, and ensures that you stay on the right path to success when it comes to managing your time, or reaching any other goal that you have.

CPSIA information can be obtained
at www.ICGtesting.com
Printed in the USA
FSHW010957100321
79362FS

9 781393 034384